New Zealand

Baby
& Toddler
Recipe
Book

Margaret Schroder

David Bateman

Thanks to Beth Davis RD, M.Ed and Michelle Hjorring B.Cap.Sc. (Hons), NZRD from Karicare for their help in the preparation of this book.

All recipes in this book have been approved by Karicare Nutricia Advisory Service Dietitians. For further help and information on infant feeding and child nutrition, please phone the Karicare dietitians toll-free on 0800-688-74242.

Published in 1996 by David Bateman Ltd, Tarndale Grove, Albany Business Park, Albany, Auckland, New Zealand

This new edition published in 1998

Cover design and illustration by Stan Mauger Design
Design by Claire Preen
Illustrations by Angela Lynskey
Printed in Hong Kong by Colorcraft Ltd

Contents

Introduction   5

Feeding Guide for Babies   6

Chapter 1
Preparation and Storage   8

Chapter 2
First Foods – 4-6 Months   12

Chapter 3
Further Progress – 6-9 Months   24

Chapter 4
Getting There – 10-12 Months   58

Chapter 5
Graduation – Over 12 Months   84

Index   115

Introduction

It is not easy to be an imaginative and creative gourmet cook when dealing with the needs of a baby or toddler. This book has been written for those wishing to give their baby a varied and nutritious diet.

Parents like to provide as wide a range of foods as their baby can tolerate. They mistakenly worry that, if given too limited a diet, their baby may refuse a well-balanced diet later on. Some parents wonder if their baby is bored by the limited selection of weaning foods. But the restricted range of pureed first foods is never dull to a baby starting on the exciting world of solid foods. Remember, he or she has just had months of nothing but milk feeds.

Parents, however, will soon become bored by what they feel is a lack of variety. This is a book full of fresh ideas and suggestions, interesting for you to cook and tasty for baby to eat. It has been written because ideas for suitable meals, snacks and desserts do not always come easily to an often over-tired mum or dad.

The book is divided into chapters beginning with Preparation and Storage of Food, followed by recipe and snack ideas according to baby's age. Recipes give both conventional and microwave cooking instructions. Recipes have been tested in a 650w microwave oven and follow the Nutricia Feeding Guide for babies.

Babies are referred to in the masculine, i.e., as 'him' and 'he', throughout this book. This is for reasons of simplicity only.

NUTRICIA

Feeding Guide for Babies

UP UNTIL 4-6 MONTHS

Breast milk or formula is all that baby needs.

AROUND 4-6 MONTHS

Baby is ready to start solids. However it is better to delay solids until nearer 6 months if there is a strong history of family allergies. Please consult your Health Professional for advice.

WHEN? When baby's appetite is clearly no longer satisfied by the milk feeds alone.

HOW? After the milk feed, smooth and creamy – free of lumps, lukewarm, slowly – one food at a time, wait 2-3 days between new foods.

WHAT? Robinsons Baby Rice; or apple, pear, nashi pear, ripe banana, apricot, peach, nectarine (remove skins) or potato, kumara, pumpkin, carrot, parsnip, swede, marrow, zucchini, avocado.

AROUND 6-7 MONTHS TRY

- lamb, chicken, beef, liver, kidney, cooked egg yolk.
- home-made gravy (mixed with vegetables or meat).
- yam, cauliflower, broccoli, taro, puha, watercress, green beans.
- watermelon, plums (remove skins and seeds).

AROUND 8-9 MONTHS

Now is the time to start offering baby solids before the milk feeds. But remember that milk is still an important part of your baby's diet. Some of these foods will still need to be modified in texture by mashing and/or finely chopping.

- fish, canned fish, tofu, legumes (such as lentils, kidney beans and chickpeas).
- luncheon/sausage (use only occasionally).
- silverbeet, spinach, peas, cabbage, tomatoes, creamed corn, onion.
- orange, kiwifruit, pineapple, berries.
- bread, pasta, wheat cereals, oatmeal, semolina, rye, barley, rusks, crackers.
- spaghetti, mashed baked beans.
- yoghurt, custard, cottage cheese, grated cheese.
- smooth peanut butter.

FOR TEETHING, OFFER
- Peeled apple, chopped carrot or a piece of frozen fruit in muslin.
- After 8 months rusks or dry toast can be used.

LEAVE UNTIL AFTER 12 MONTHS
Cow's milk as a primary drink, adult muesli, honey, egg white, shellfish, pork.

After 12 months, baby can join in with family meals and eat a wide variety of foods.

DELAY UNTIL 12 MONTHS IF ALLERGIES RUN IN THE FAMILY
Cow's milk, cheese, yoghurt, tofu, wheat, rye, oats, barley, egg white, fish, citrus fruit, strawberries, tomato, chocolate, peanut butter.

REMEMBER
- If extra fluids are needed in addition to breast milk or formula, use water.
- Leave out bad habit formers such as added salt, sweets and salty snack foods.
- To help prevent choking, avoid small hard foods such as peanuts, pretzels and popcorn.

For further advice speak to one of our dietitians by calling

Toll Free on: 0800 NUTRICIA

0800 688 74242

1

Preparation and Storage

PREPARATION

Because it takes some time for a baby's digestive system to build up an immunity to household germs, extra care must be taken with food preparation. This is important as a baby suffering from diarrhoea or vomiting due to an intestinal infection is at greater risk from dehydration.

In this chapter, we look at preparing and handling food in a safe manner. Bacteria need food, water and the correct temperature to grow. To keep food safe, bacteria numbers must be reduced as much as possible, and their environment rendered too unpleasant for further multiplication.

Always wash your hands with soap before preparing meals. If you are interrupted or called away to another task, don't leave food uncovered on the bench. Pop it into the fridge until you return, and re-wash your hands before continuing. Keep all prepared food covered and stored in the fridge and use within 24 hours. If leftovers are used, re-heat them only once. Do not keep any leftovers that have contained spoons with baby's saliva on them. The traces of saliva start bacterial breakdown.

When preparing baby's food, scrub and scald can-openers and chopping boards to remove all traces of previous food. Use clean kitchen knives and spoons. Thoroughly wash all utensils, including food processors and blenders. Simply rinsing them off with water doesn't do much other than re-arrange the germs.

Where possible, take mechanisms apart and check for trapped food.

Automatic dishwashers are good for cleaning baby's special cups, dishes and spoons, but it is necessary to ensure the water temperature gets up to 42°C, and that a thorough rinse cycle removes all traces of caustic detergent. As tea towels harbour many germs, use a fresh one for baby's dishes. Watch out for food catching in the spouts of Tommee Tippee cups. Wash them out thoroughly with soap and hot water,.

Eventually your young baby's digestive system will build up a resistance to the ever-present germs. In the meantime, a sensible level of care is required to avoid any disturbing "tummy upsets".

STORAGE

Fresh Food

Fruit and vegetable purees should be stored in the fridge for no more than 3 days. Ideally, they should be eaten straight away and leftovers discarded. Meals prepared with breast milk or formula should be kept for no more than 24 hours. Bacteria multiply rapidly in milk, particularly warm milk. Never leave a bottle of cow's milk or prepared formula sitting on a bench for any period. If you do, throw it away. Do not re-chill. It's not worth the risk.

Young babies require very small tastes of food – sometimes only a teaspoon at a time. This is why packaged baby cereals – like the Robinsons range – are ideal for beginners. Not only are they fortified with valuable nutrients, but they store well.

Likewise, cans and jars of baby dinners are good for convenience and storage. They contain approximately the same nutritional value as your homecooked dinner, and are ideal for travelling and visiting. Use commercial baby foods as a base, as they are excellent to add to fruit or vegetables to produce more texture when baby gets older.

Frozen Food

The fruit and vegetable purees, soups and stews recommended in Chapters 2 and 3 often make more than is required. They can be safely frozen and thawed later using the following method. Do not freeze food for longer than four weeks.

Pour excess food into an ice block tray and freeze it immediately. When frozen, remove from iceblock tray and pack into a small, very clean plastic bag. Seal bag with a twist tie, and label it with the date. Return bag to freezer until required. One iceblock is usually sufficient for first meals, gradually increasing to two or three.

When frozen food is to be used, heat to boiling point on stove or in microwave. Cool and serve. Do not re-freeze leftovers from previously frozen food. It is safer to throw them away.

By using this method of storage, it is not necessary to cook and puree food for baby's every meal. A selection of three or four different purees can be kept frozen and prepared quickly and conveniently.

Free-flow Method

Various commercially prepared finger foods mentioned can be conveniently frozen free-flow, so that one or two may be used at a time. Cheerios and crumpets come into this category. Fish cakes, fish fingers and oven fries generally come packaged already free-flow.

Place food in a medium-sized clean plastic bag and fasten with a twist tie. Place in freezer overnight. Next morning, remove bag from freezer and scrunch food (through plastic) with fingers to separate any items stuck together. Return bag to freezer, label with the date and store until required.

2

First Foods

4-6 Months

Semi-solid foods are introduced from 4-6 months of age. In these early days of feeding solids, the tongue frequently pushes out most of the food that goes in on the spoon. This makes feeding infants not only messy but frustrating too. By mastering the act of moving food from the front of the tongue to the back, your baby is learning how to chew rather than suck his food.

Babies ready for solids have lost the extrusion reflex which causes infant tongues to push solid food back out. As their skills develop, babies begin to sit with balance and to reach for and grasp objects. Other signs of readiness also appear, such as opening the mouth and leaning forward to show a desire for food. Solids should not be introduced before 4 months as the gut and kidneys are too immature.

Solid food must be introduced gradually and in very small amounts. Milk remains a baby's most important food, and solids should always be given after a milk feed. Begin with no more than 1-2 teaspoons of food, gradually increasing the amount as he or she becomes used to it. It is recommended to start weaning with Baby Rice, then try new foods one at a time, staying with it for 2-3 days before introducing another. Once your baby is used to simple tastes, interesting combinations can be tried.

First foods need to be prepared to a semi-liquid consistency with a food processor, blender or mouli. Babies do not like swallowing pips, lumps, or stringy skins, so take time to puree or sieve first foods thoroughly. At around 7 months, food can be mashed with a fork or potato masher. Salt and sugar do not need to be added. Indeed, excess use can cause health problems in young babies and can contribute to health problems in later years. Don't substitute honey for sugar.

HOT TIP: If baby is under 6 months old and being fed on formula, use infant formula in these recipes, NOT a Follow-On formula. Karicare Follow-On formula is designed for babies over 6 months.

REMEMBER: Always check the temperature of cooked food before feeding it to baby. Beware of microwave "hot-spots".

First Foods
Index

Apple, Banana and Kumara Delight   21

Apple Puree   16

Apricot, Peach and Pear Purees   16

Avocado and Banana Mash   22

Baby Rice   15

Banana Mush   17

Buttercup and Swede   18

Combination Vegie Soup   19

Creamy Vegies and Rice   20

Kumara and Carrot   18

Mashed Potato and Gravy   18

Pumpkin and Herb Soup   19

Pumpkin Smash   17

Robinsons and Fruit   17

Robinsons Royale   15

Suggested Finger Foods   23

Summer Fruit Salad   22

Three Vegie Treat   19

Baby Rice

Cereals are usually baby's first solid food. Commercially prepared infant cereals, such as Robinsons Baby Rice, are ideal because they are enriched with vitamins and minerals, particularly iron.

1 heaped teaspoon Robinsons Baby Rice
2 teaspoons cooled boiled water/expressed breast milk/infant
   formula

In a small bowl or cup, mix cereal with water or milk to a runny paste. Adjust consistency, and increase amounts as baby grows.

Robinsons Royale

1 tablespoon Robinsons Baby Rice
2 tablespoons expressed breast milk/cooled boiled water/infant
   formula
1 tablespoon pureed banana or other suitable fruit
   (see Feeding Guide)

Combine all ingredients thoroughly in a small bowl or cup and serve . . . delicious.

Fruit Purees

The most suitable fruits for a 4-6 month old are apple, pear, ripe banana, apricot, peach and nectarine. All should be pureed in these initial stages. Some fruit may need to be stewed first. Do not add sugar – baby doesn't need it.

Apple Puree

1 medium cooking apple
$^3/_4$ cup water

Peel, core and chop apple into fine slices.

MICROWAVE: Place apple in water and cook on HIGH for 3-4 minutes or until tender.

CONVENTIONAL: Simmer apple in water in a small saucepan until it is soft.

BOTH: Allow to cool. Puree in food blender or strain through mouli. Consistency should be semi-liquid. If it's too stiff, add some cooled boiled water.

HOT TIP: This makes more than baby needs so freeze what's left in ice block trays as outlined in Chapter 1.

Apricot, Peach and Pear Purees

Replace apple with a pear, a couple of small apricots or a peach in the above recipe.

Banana Mush

¹/₂ very ripe banana
1 tablespoon breast milk/infant formula

Thoroughly mash or puree banana and milk together to a runny paste. For babies six months and over, Robinsons Egg Custard is a nice addition to this recipe.

Pumpkin Smash

1 cup peeled and diced pumpkin
enough water to cover

MICROWAVE: Place pumpkin in water and cook on HIGH for 5 minutes until pumpkin is soft, stirring occasionally.

CONVENTIONAL: Boil pumpkin in water until it is just tender.

BOTH: Allow to cool. Puree in food blender or sieve until smooth.

HOT TIP: As baby grows older, use less water for a firmer texture.

BABY BONUS: Freeze unused portion in ice block trays as explained in Chapter 1.

Mashed Potato and Gravy

1 tablespoon mashed potato
1 tablespoon home-made gravy

Mix to a semi-liquid paste and serve. Substitute vegetable water for gravy if you're not having gravy for your tea.

Kumara and Carrot

1 medium kumara, peeled and diced
1 small carrot, peeled and diced
water to cover

Combine ingredients in a small microwave bowl or a saucepan.

MICROWAVE: Cook on HIGH for 5 minutes or until tender, stirring twice.

CONVENTIONAL: Simmer in saucepan until soft.

BOTH: Allow to cool. Put through blender or mouli.

HOT TIP: Makes more than baby needs for first meals. Freeze in ice block trays as outlined in Chapter 1.

Buttercup and Swede

1 medium piece buttercup pumpkin, peeled and diced
1 small piece swede, peeled and chopped

Prepare as for *Kumara and Carrot.*

Three Vegie Treat

Once baby is happy with simple tastes, interesting combinations can be tried.

Take three vegetables from your own dinner (any of those in previous recipes are suitable). Mix with a little vegetable water, breast milk or infant formula, and puree.

Pumpkin and Herb Soup

$^1/_4$ cup mashed pumpkin
$^1/_4$ cup cooled boiled water
1 pinch chopped fresh herbs – parsley, chives, basil, etc.

Combine all ingredients in blender or food processor. Reheat to boiling in microwave or saucepan. Allow to cool.

Combination Vegie Soup

Take any combination of the following cooked vegetables from the family meal: potato, carrot, swede, pumpkin, marrow, kumara.

1 tablespoon each vegetable
1 cup vegetable water

Puree ingredients together. For very young babies, strain out any lumps through a sieve. Reheat to serving temperature if necessary.

Creamy Vegies and Rice

1 medium potato
1 medium piece of pumpkin
1 carrot
2 bay leaves
water to cover
1-2 tablespoons Robinsons Baby Rice
50 ml breast milk/cooled boiled water/infant formula

Peel and dice vegetables. Combine vegetables and bay leaves in a small microwave dish or saucepan. Cover with water.

MICROWAVE: Cook on HIGH for 8-10 minutes or until vegetables are tender, stirring twice.

CONVENTIONAL: Simmer in saucepan until vegetables are tender.

BOTH: Drain water and remove bay leaves. Blend or mouli vegetables until smooth. Mix Robinsons Baby Rice with milk or water, varying the amount of rice according to how thick you want the puree. Add rice mixture into the vegetable puree.

HOT TIP: Makes more than baby will need. Freeze in ice block trays as outlined in Chapter 1.

Apple, Banana and Kumara Delight

Cinnamon gives a lift to the kumara. This is a simple recipe to make.

1 medium kumara
water to cover
2 tablespoons Robinsons Apple and Banana Cereal
50 ml breast milk/infant formula
¼ teaspoon cinnamon

Peel kumara and cut into chunks. Place in a small microwave bowl or saucepan together with water.

MICROWAVE: Cook on HIGH for 5-7 minutes until tender. Stir once.

CONVENTIONAL: Simmer until soft.

BOTH: Drain. Add breast milk/formula to kumara and mash until soft. Add Robinsons Apple and Banana Cereal and cinnamon to the mashed kumara. Blend well.

Summer Fruit Salad

1 medium apple or pear
³/₄ cup water
1 tablespoon Robinsons Summer Fruit Salad

Peel, core and chop apple or pear. Place in a a small microwave bowl or saucepan together with water.

MICROWAVE: Cook on HIGH for 3-4 minutes until soft, stirring once.

CONVENTIONAL: Simmer until tender.

BOTH: Puree with the cooking liquid. Blend in Robinsons Summer Fruit Salad.

Avocado and Banana Mash

¹/₂ very ripe avocado
¹/₂ ripe banana

Scoop flesh into a small cup or bowl and mash. Thin to a runny paste with a little cooled boiled water, breast milk or infant formula. Press through sieve to remove any lumps and fibres. For older babies, serve thicker and without sieving.

SUGGESTED FINGER FOODS

Fruit in Muslin

1 wedge of apple or other firm fruit
small circular piece muslin cloth (about the size of a saucer)
    length of sewing cotton

Place apple in centre of muslin circle. Gather up edges and tie securely with cotton, forming a money-bag shape. Show baby how to hold the tied end while sucking fruit pulp through the cloth.

Simply Carrot

1 raw carrot

Peel a four inch piece of carrot, wrap in muslin to avoid choking, and give to baby to suck.

Drumstick Lick

1 chicken drumstick bone

Remove any loose meat or gristle from drumstick. Give bone to baby to suck. Wrap in muslin to avoid choking.

3

Further Progress

6-9 Months

After six months of age, breast milk or formula alone is not sufficient for baby's continued optimal growth. Therefore, it is important that baby is introduced to foods other than milk. However, new foods need to be offered at the right stage of baby's development. Some foods introduced too early can be damaging to baby's health.

For example, unmodified cow's milk plays an important role in building strong bones and teeth, but it shouldn't be used as a main drink before 12 months of age. Unmodified cow's milk contains too little iron, too much protein, as well as minerals such as sodium, potassium and chloride, which burden immature kidneys. If cow's milk is introduced too early, intestinal irritation and iron deficiency can result.

If not breastfeeding, health professionals recommend a FOLLOW-ON FORMULA rather than cow's milk, which meets all the energy, protein, vitamin and mineral needs of older infants.

Follow-On milk formula can be made up according to manufacturer's instructions and stored in the fridge for up to 24 hours. Store the formula at the back of the fridge where it will not be subject to fluctuating temperatures due to the opening and closing of the door. It can be given as the main source of milk and/or used in recipes for babies up to 24 months of age.

Around 6-7 months chicken, liver, lamb, kidney, beef, egg yolk and many vegetables can be introduced into baby's diet. Bread, pasta, wheat-containing cereals, fish, citrus fruit, yoghurt and cheese can be introduced around 8 months.

Many babies find they no longer need their solid food pureed to such a fine degree. Mashing with a fork or potato masher will produce a coarser texture that baby will find quite interesting. Previous recipes can continue to be used if not so finely strained. The amount of solids given should be increased according to your baby's appetite. After 8 months, solids should be given before the milk feed.

If allergies run in the family, avoid cow's milk, cheese, yoghurt, wheat-containing cereals, fish, citrus fruit, tomatoes, strawberries, chocolate and peanuts until baby is over 12 months.

REMEMBER: You should always check the temperature of cooked food before feeding it to baby. Be aware of microwave "hot-spots".

Further Progress
Index

Apricot and Orange Vegies	29
Apricot Shake	45
Baby Roast Dinner	36
Banana Shake	43
Beef Noodle Soup	38
Beef and Vegetable Stew	35
Blackcurrant Jelly	42
Braised Liver and Baby Bacon	33
Cheeky Chicken	32
Cheesy Potatoes	40
Chicken and Sweetcorn Soup	39
Chicken and Vegetable Stew	34
Chicken Noodle Soup	38
Chocolate Semolina	41
Chocolate Shake	45
Combination Vegie Extra	28
Corned Beef and Vegetable Stew	35
Country Custard	44
Creamy Tutti-Frutti	44
Egg Yolk Supreme	28

Frozen Banana	42
Fruity Summer Salad	46
Ham and Vegetable Soup	38
Herbed Spaghetti Treat	36
Island Delight	43
Jolly Jelly	42
Kidney and Vegetable Surprise	31
Lamb and Vegetable Stew	34
Liver and Baby Bacon Delight	40
Liver and Vegetable Casserole	35
Meat and Vegetable Bake	33
Party Pumpkin	30
Pasta'n'Sauce	37
Perfect Parfait	46
Semolina Pudding	41
Simply Spaghetti	37
Soft-Boiled Egg Yolk	28
Suggested Finger Foods	47
Suggested Snacks	55
Tomato and Cheese Soup	39
Vanilla Shake	45
Yoghurt and Fruit	43

Combination Vegie Extra

At 6-7 months, egg yolk can be introduced into baby's diet. Do not give egg white until baby is at least 12 months of age.

1 hard-boiled egg yolk
3-4 cooked vegetables
vegetable water, breast milk or formula to mix

Add cooked egg yolk to vegetables before pureeing.

Egg Yolk Supreme

1 hard-boiled egg yolk
a little boiled vegetable water (cooled)

Mash yolk and stir in enough water to create a runny paste. Breast milk or formula can be substituted for vegetable water for variety.

Soft-Boiled Egg Yolk

1 medium egg

Bring saucepan of water to the boil. Gently ease raw egg into water, taking care it doesn't crack. Boil three minutes for a runny yolk. Allow to cool. Slice open top and feed only yolk to baby.

Apricot and Orange Vegies

2 medium carrots
1 large potato
1 cup water
2 tablespoons Robinsons Apricot and Orange Semolina
50 ml breast milk/Karicare Follow-On milk

Peel and dice vegetables. Place in a small microwave bowl or saucepan together with water.

MICROWAVE: Cook on HIGH for 8-10 minutes until tender, stirring twice.

CONVENTIONAL: Simmer until well-cooked.

BOTH: Drain. Add milk to cooked vegetables and mash. Add Robinsons Apricot and Orange Semolina according to how thick you want the mashed vegetables. Allow to cool before serving.

Party Pumpkin

1 medium piece pumpkin
1 zucchini
1 tablespoon orange juice
2 tablespoons Robinsons Muesli

Peel pumpkin and dice vegetables. Place in a small microwave bowl or saucepan covered with a little water.

MICROWAVE: Cook on HIGH for 5-7 minutes until soft, stirring once.

CONVENTIONAL: Simmer vegetables until tender.

BOTH: Drain. Mash vegetables with orange juice. Add Robinsons Muesli and blend well. Cool and serve.

Once baby is accustomed to cereals, fruits and vegetables, meats can be introduced into the diet, usually at around 6-7 months.

Kidney and Vegetable Surprise

1 medium potato or kumara
2 small carrots
1 medium piece pumpkin
1 sheep's kidney (frozen)

Peel vegetables and chop into chunks. Place in medium-sized microwave bowl or saucepan. Barely cover with water.

MICROWAVE: Cook on HIGH for 10 minutes, stirring 2-3 times.

CONVENTIONAL: Simmer until vegetables are cooked but still firm.

BOTH: Grate frozen kidney into vegetables. Continue to cook for a further 5 minutes, until the grated kidney turns a chocolate colour. (Potato or kumara may discolour slightly.) Mash together with cooking water.

HOT TIP: Makes more than one meal. Freeze unused portion in ice cube trays as explained in Chapter 1.

BABY BONUS: To start with, you may want to use ½ kidney and increase this as your baby enjoys it.

Cheeky Chicken

50 grams chicken – cooked and diced
$1/4$ cup cooked rice
1 ripe peach – peeled and diced
1 tablespoon peach juice or orange juice
1 tablespoon Karicare Follow-On milk
1 tablespoon Robinsons Summer Fruit Salad

Mix all ingredients together thoroughly. Warm through in microwave or over low heat. Serve.

BABY BONUS: *Cheeky Chicken* is delicious served hot. Alternatively, it can be served cold, ensuring ingredients are first cooked thoroughly as noted above.

Braised Liver and Baby Bacon

Liver is an excellent source of iron and other minerals.

1 slice lamb's fry
$^1/_2$ slice lean ham, rind removed
1 medium potato, peeled and cubed
$^3/_4$ cup water

Gently poach liver and potato in hot water until just cooked. Either microwave ham on HIGH for 30 seconds or poach with liver. Allow to cool. Puree combined ingredients to a semi-liquid state.

Meat and Vegetable Bake

30g finely diced beef or lamb
1 small zucchini – washed and sliced
1 small carrot – washed and sliced
2 broccoli or cauliflower florets
1 small kumara – peeled and diced
1 egg yolk
$^1/_4$ cup cheddar cheese – grated

Place meat and vegetables in a medium-sized microwave bowl or saucepan. Barely cover with water.

MICROWAVE: Cook on HIGH for 8-10 minutes until meat is cooked and vegetables are soft.

CONVENTIONAL: Simmer until meat is brown and vegetables are tender.

BOTH: Allow to cool slightly. Puree with cooking water. Add egg yolk and cheese. Bake in a greased dish at 180°C (350°F) for 15 minutes.

Chicken and Vegetable Stew

2 tablespoons well-cooked diced chicken
$^1/_2$ carrot
$^1/_2$ zucchini
1 small kumara or sweet potato
$^3/_4$ cup water

Peel and dice vegetables. Place in small bowl or saucepan with water.

MICROWAVE: Cook on HIGH 5-7 minutes or until tender.

CONVENTIONAL: Simmer vegetables in saucepan until soft.

BOTH: Add cooked meat. Bring back to the boil. Remove from heat and allow to cool. Process through food mouli or blender. Recipe can be doubled and remainder frozen for future meals as explained in Chapter 1.

Lamb and Vegetable Stew

2 tablespoons well-cooked diced lamb
1 piece pumpkin
1 piece sweet potato or kumara
1 floret broccoli
$^3/_4$ cup water

Prepare and cook as for *Chicken and Vegetable Stew.*

Corned Beef and Vegetable Stew

2 tablespoons well-cooked diced corned beef
1 medium potato
1 floret cauliflower
1 small leaf silverbeet or spinach
$^3/_4$ cup water

Prepare and cook as for *Chicken and Vegetable Stew.*

Beef and Vegetable Stew

2 tablespoons well-cooked diced beef (steak, roast beef, pot roast)
1 medium potato
$^1/_2$ carrot
$^1/_2$ parsnip
$^3/_4$ cup water

Prepare and cook as for *Chicken and Vegetable Stew.*

Liver and Vegetable Casserole

2 tablespoons cooked diced liver
$^1/_2$ carrot
1 floret cauliflower
1 small kumara or sweet potato
$^3/_4$ cup water

Prepare and cook as for *Chicken and Vegetable Stew.*

Baby Roast Dinner

This one's the quickest and easiest yet. From your own roast dinner take:

> 2 tablespoons well-cooked meat
> 1 small piece of each vegetable
> $\frac{1}{2}$ cup thin gravy (or vegetable water)

Puree all ingredients in blender or processor until smooth. Add a little extra gravy or vegetable water as necessary.

BABY BONUS: Amounts can be increased and surplus frozen as outlined in Chapter 1.

HOT TIP: Baby may now be able to tolerate small lumps, so you may not need to puree food to such a fine degree.

Herbed Spaghetti Treat

> $\frac{1}{2}$ cup cooked spaghetti
> 1 teaspoon flour
> 100 ml Karicare Follow-On milk formula
> $\frac{1}{4}$ teaspoon each finely chopped parsley and chives

Cut spaghetti into baby bite-sized pieces. Stir flour into freshly cooked and drained spaghetti. Add milk and herbs. Stir to combine.

MICROWAVE: Cook mixture $1\frac{1}{2}$-2 minutes on HIGH – stirring twice – until it boils and thickens.

CONVENTIONAL: Heat mixture through, stirring to prevent sticking.

BOTH: Allow to cool.

Simply Spaghetti

$^1/_2$ cup spaghetti and home-made tomato sauce

MICROWAVE: Cook on HIGH until heated through.

CONVENTIONAL: Stir in saucepan until heated through.

BOTH: Allow to cool. Cut spaghetti into bite-sized pieces with edge of spoon while feeding.

Pasta'n'Sauce

$^1/_2$ cup cooked fettucine noodles
1 teaspoon margarine or butter
1 teaspoon standard flour
100 ml Karicare Follow-On milk formula
2 tablespoons grated cheese

MICROWAVE: In a small microwave-safe bowl or jug, melt butter on HIGH 10 seconds. Stir in flour. Add milk and whisk until smooth. Cook 1 minute on HIGH, then stir. Cook a further 20-30 seconds until boiling. Watch sauce doesn't boil over. Stir in cheese until melted.

CONVENTIONAL: Melt butter in saucepan. Stir in flour and milk. Bring to the boil and cook one minute, stirring constantly. Add cheese and stir until melted.

BOTH: Stir in cooked and drained fettucine. Chop noodles into bite-sized pieces with a sharp knife against the edge of the dish before serving.

Chicken Noodle Soup

$1/_2$ cup home-made chicken stock
(or chicken stock made with:
$1/_2$ cup boiling water
$1/_2$ teaspoon chicken stock powder)
$1/_2$ cup cooked noodles
1 teaspoon finely chopped parsley

Combine drained noodles, chicken stock and parsley. Bring to boil either in microwave or on stovetop. Allow to cool. Chop egg noodles into baby bite-sized pieces with a sharp knife against the edge of the cup or dish before serving.

Beef Noodle Soup

Substitute $1/_2$ cup beef stock for chicken in above recipe.

Ham and Vegetable Soup

1 ham bone or slice of ham
1 small potato
1 piece pumpkin
1 other suitable vegetable (carrot, parsnip, silverbeet etc)
2 cups water

Peel and dice vegetables. Dice ham slice if used. Place ingredients in water, bring to the boil, then simmer 30 minutes. Remove bone if used. Allow to cool before pulping in blender or food processor. Add a little boiled water if too thick.

Tomato and Cheese Soup

1 large ripe tomato (or 2 small tomatoes)
boiling water
$^1/_2$ cup water
1 tablespoon grated cheese

Plunge tomato into boiling water to help remove skin. Peel, core and chop tomato.

MICROWAVE: Cook tomato in water 2 minutes on HIGH.

CONVENTIONAL: Put tomato in water and bring to the boil in saucepan. Remove from heat after boiling tomato 1 minute.

BOTH: Stir in cheese until melted. Allow to cool slightly and puree in blender. Reheat to serving temperature if too cool. Do not freeze. Do not store leftovers longer than 24 hours.

Chicken and Sweetcorn Soup

2 tablespoons creamed-style sweetcorn
$^3/_4$ cup water
$^1/_2$ teaspoon chicken stock
(can be made with 1 cup of home-made chicken stock if
    available)

Combine ingredients. No added salt is necessary.

MICROWAVE: Cook on HIGH 4 minutes until boiling.

CONVENTIONAL: Boil mixture 4 minutes.

BOTH: Once cool, liquidize in blender or food processor. Strain through sieve to remove lumps.

Liver and Baby Bacon Delight

1 small piece lamb's fry
$^1/_2$ slice lean ham – rind removed
1 teaspoon margarine
1 teaspoon home-made gravy
$^1/_3$ cup water

Cut lamb's fry and ham into small cubes. Melt butter in frying pan. Cook liver and ham until well browned and pink juices have turned clear. Remove cooked meat from pan. Stir gravy mix into water and pour into pan. Stir until gravy boils and thickens, scraping cooked juices from bottom of frypan at the same time. Return meat to pan. Allow to cool and blend in food processor to reduce meat to a suitable consistency.

HOT TIP: Provide baby with fingers of toast dipped into liver mixture in between spoonfuls. Encourage baby to feed himself as much as possible.

BABY BONUS: *Liver and Baby Bacon Delight* is so delicious, why not cook enough for the whole family, pulping only baby's portion?

Cheesy Potatoes

$^1/_2$ cup mashed potatoes
2 tablespoons grated cheese
$^1/_4$ teaspoon finely chopped parsley

Combine ingredients. Add a little milk or vegetable water if mixture seems too thick.

HOT TIP: Heat from the potatoes will melt the cheese.

Semolina Pudding

Semolina is made from ground wheat and is readily available from most supermarkets. It can be used in a variety of tasty milk puddings that baby will love.

    150 ml Karicare Follow-On milk formula
    2 tablespoons semolina
    1 tablespoon fruit puree

Combine all ingredients in a small bowl or saucepan.

MICROWAVE: Cook $2^{1}/_{2}$-3 minutes on HIGH, stirring several times, until mixture boils and thickens.

CONVENTIONAL: Bring to boil, stirring often to prevent mixture sticking to bottom of saucepan.

BOTH: Allow to stand. Thickens while cooling.

Chocolate Semolina

Add 1 teaspoon cocoa to *Semolina Pudding* recipe.

Frozen Banana

What to do with those banana halves left over from other recipes.

$^1/_2$ banana
3 wooden ice block sticks

Cut banana into three thick circles. Carefully press an iceblock stick into the middle of each circle. Freeze bananas overnight. Give to baby to suck.

BABY BONUS: Also ideal as a food for older children with sore throats.

Jolly Jelly

50 ml hot water
1 teaspoon gelatine
50 ml fruit juice

Dissolve gelatine in slightly cooled boiled water. Stir into fruit juice. Pour into small jelly mould or custard cup. Leave in fridge to set. Unmould onto plate before feeding to baby.

HOT TIP: To unmould jelly without ruining shape, stand jelly mould in a dish of hot water for 1 minute to loosen.

Blackcurrant Jelly

Substitute 50 ml Ribena for fruit juice in above recipe.

HOT TIP: Ribena blackcurrant drink is available in convenient-sized packs from most supermarkets and dairies.

Yoghurt and Fruit

$^1/_2$ cup commercially prepared natural yoghurt
3 tablespoons stewed fruit
(fresh or frozen as outlined in Chapter 1)
Combine yoghurt and stewed fruit and serve.

Banana Shake

150 ml Karicare Follow-On milk formula
$^1/_2$ very ripe banana

Mash banana thoroughly. Put into shaker with the milk and shake well to combine. Banana fibres will not pass through holes in Tommee Tippee, so help baby drink from a cup. Or, put the banana and milk into a blender to make a delicious "smoothie"(see Chapter 4 – page 75 for alternative recipe).

Island Delight

$^1/_2$ avocado
$^1/_2$ small banana
1 tablespoon plain yoghurt
1 tablespoon Robinsons Apple and Banana Cereal

Scoop flesh out of avocado and mash with banana. Mix in yoghurt and Robinsons Apple and Banana Cereal. Serve.

Creamy Tutti-Frutti

1 ripe peach or pear
2 tablespoons plain yoghurt
2 tablespoons cottage cheese
1 tablespoon Robinsons Muesli

Peel, core and mash fruit. Blend in yoghurt, cottage cheese and Robinsons Muesli. Serve.

Country Custard

1 medium apple – peeled and diced
2 prunes – chopped
3 tablespoons Robinsons Egg Custard
cinnamon and nutmeg

Place apple and prunes in a small microwave bowl or saucepan. Cover with a little water.

MICROWAVE: Cook on HIGH for 5-7 minutes until apple is soft.

CONVENTIONAL: Simmer until fruit is tender.

BOTH: Mash in cooking juices. Blend in Robinsons Egg Custard and a pinch of each spice. Cool and serve.

Serve the following drinks in a Tommee Tippee cup at first, graduating to a glass and straw later on.

Apricot Shake

150 ml Karicare Follow-On milk formula
3 tablespoons apricot puree (or any other fruit puree)
   (fresh or thawed as outlined in Chapter 1)

Put ingredients into lidded shaker (or any container with a firm fitting lid). Shake well to combine.

Vanilla Shake

150 ml Karicare Follow-On milk formula
2-3 drops vanilla essence

Put ingredients into lidded shaker and shake well to combine.

Chocolate Shake

150 ml Karicare Follow-On milk formula
1 teaspoon Milo
1 tablespoon boiling water

Dissolve Milo in boiling water. Put all ingredients into lidded shaker and shake well to combine.

Fruity Summer Salad

$^1/_2$ soft peach or nectarine – peeled and diced
4 strawberries – hulled and diced
1 pottle fruit salad yoghurt
2 tablespoons fruit juice
3 tablespoons Robinsons Summer Fruit Salad

Mix all ingredients together until well blended. Serve.

Perfect Parfait

6 tablespoons Robinsons Apricot and Orange Semolina
6 tablespoons water
1 pottle apricot yoghurt
1 orange
1 teaspoon gelatine
$^1/_4$ cup boiling water
$^1/_4$ cup fruit juice

Mix together Robinsons Apricot and Orange Semolina and water. Place into bottom of 2 small parfait dishes or small glasses. Place yoghurt on top of mixture. Cut orange into small pieces and place on top of yoghurt. Mix boiling water and juice together. Sprinkle gelatine over hot juice mixture and stir until dissolved. Chill until partially set. Place on top of orange pieces. Chill again until set. Serves 2 toddlers.

SUGGESTED FINGER FOODS

Finger Foods are great for busy parents. They enable baby or toddler to get on with feeding himself, thus increasing both his independence and your spare time. You can get on with other tasks nearby while keeping a small supply of interesting tidbits on baby's high chair tray. Entire meals – particularly lunches – can be made up from finger foods and still provide a nutritionally balanced meal.

While still nourishing, first finger foods are really good for educating baby about how to hold and suck. He learns that food tastes nicer than plastic toys. Later he will learn that sucking on finger foods actually satisfies his hunger.

Never leave baby unattended while eating, as babies and toddlers have a higher risk of choking than older children. It's easily avoided, however, if you take some simple precautions:

- Avoid foods that are hard to control in the mouth such as nuts, small pieces of raw carrot and lollies.

- Modify some foods, e.g., quarter Cheerios and frankfurters lengthwise, quarter and de-pip grapes, cook carrots.

- Always remain with baby while he's eating.

- Keep baby seated while eating. Most choking occurs when toddlers eat on the run.

Choking is not the same as gagging. All children gag. It's their protection when they are learning to chew and swallow. The gagging reflex helps to propel food back out. Baby will not get excited or upset by this unless you do.

REMEMBER: Always check the temperature of cooked food before feeding it to baby. Beware of microwave "hot-spots"

Around 6-7 months :

Grated Goodies

2 tablespoons grated carrot
2 tablespoons grated apple
2 tablespoons grated zucchini

Place grated goodies on high chair tray. If you use a plate, baby will most likely tip them off anyway. Leave him to feed himself. (Grated cheese can be included at 8 months).

Roast Vegetables

A selection of roast vegetables from the family meal.

Give baby a whole piece of each roast vegetable – one at a time – to pick up and suck. Roast vegetables are soft enough not to choke on, but don't leave baby unattended while eating. Baby loves the challenge of feeding himself.

Kumara Sticks

1 medium kumara or sweet potato
2 teaspoons oil

Peel kumara and cut into 1 cm thick sticks. Brush with oil.

MICROWAVE: Place in shallow dish. Cook on HIGH 4-5 minutes turning 2 or 3 times.

CONVENTIONAL: Place in baking dish. Bake 20 minutes at 200°C turning occasionally.

BOTH: Drain on paper towel.

Potato Wedges

1 medium potato (unpeeled but well scrubbed)
1 tablespoon oil
1 pinch low-sodium green herb stock (if desired)

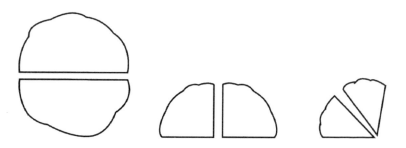

Cut potato in half lengthwise, then each half lengthwise again. Quarters should be cut diagonally lengthwise as shown in diagrams, to produce 8 even-sized wedges.

MICROWAVE: Cook oil 10 seconds on HIGH. Place wedges on plate and brush with warm oil. Cook on HIGH 3 minutes. Turn wedges over and brush with oil again. Cook on HIGH a further 2 minutes.

CONVENTIONAL: Brush warm oil over wedges. Grill one side 5 minutes. Turn over and brush other side with oil. Grill a further 5 minutes. Turn one last time and grill 5 minutes more.

BOTH: Sprinkle with herb stock if desired.

HOT TIP: Can be used as an accompaniment to meals.

Around 8-9 months :

Vegetable Platter

As with fruit, some vegetables need to be peeled and lightly boiled – firm enough for baby to pick up, but soft enough to suck on and swallow.

Arrange a selection of sliced vegetables on baby's high chair tray. Try lightly boiled carrot sticks, potato or kumara wedges, parsnip circles, turnip sticks, beans, or peas (a real challenge for little fingers). Baby should be able to manage peeled tomato wedges without cooking.

HOT TIP: 2 tablespoons of cooked frozen mixed vegetables add colour and variety to platter.

Fruit Platter

Platters give baby plenty of variety and allow him to choose his own order of eating. At this age, some fruit needs to be peeled and lightly stewed – firm enough for baby to pick up, but soft enough to suck on and swallow. Remember, baby may have only a few teeth.

Arrange a selection of lightly stewed or very ripe fruit slices on baby's high chair tray. Try peach, pear, apple and apricot. Baby should be able to manage softer fruits such as pawpaw, watermelon, banana, peeled and pipped grapes, orange, nectarines or mandarins without stewing.

Super Sandwiches

2 slices bread with crusts removed
margarine if desired
filling – Marmite, cheese spread, pate, spaghetti,
    mashed baked beans, mashed banana etc.

Spread one slice of bread with margarine and filling. Top with second slice of bread. Cut into four triangles. Cut each triangle in half again.

BABY BONUS: These sandwiches are just the right size for baby to pick up and eat.

Cheerios

Keep Cheerios (or cocktail sausages) frozen "free-flow". See Chapter 1 for free-flow method.

2-3 Cheerios
water to cover
1 tablespoon tomato sauce (if desired)

MICROWAVE: Put Cheerios and water in bowl. Cook 1-2 minutes on HIGH (1 minute longer for frozen Cheerios) until water boils and sausages are heated through. Allow to cool.

CONVENTIONAL: Bring Cheerios and water to the boil. Simmer 2 or 3 minutes until sausages are heated through. Allow to cool.

BOTH: Remove skins from Cheerios. These will be too tough for tiny teeth until around 18 months. Cut Cheerios into quarters lengthwise. Show baby how to dip Cheerio into tomato sauce for added flavour if desired.

Fish Fingers

A box of commercially prepared fish fingers in the freezer comes in handy for both Finger Foods and Fish and Chips Meals.

> 2 fish fingers
> 1 tablespoon tomato sauce (if desired)

MICROWAVE: Place frozen fish fingers on a plate. Cook 30 seconds on HIGH. Turn over. Cook a further 30 seconds.

CONVENTIONAL: Place fish fingers under griller. Cook 2 or 3 minutes each side.

BOTH: Serve either whole or cut into bite-sized pieces – with tomato sauce if desired.

Rollups

> 1 slice bread
> margarine if desired
> filling – Marmite, cheese spread, pate, spaghetti,
>   mashed baked beans, mashed banana etc.

Cut crusts off bread. Spread with margarine and filling, ensuring a thickish layer of filling along one edge. Roll up bread towards extra filling which is used to hold rollup closed. Cut roll in half crosswise and then into quarters to make four pinwheel-shaped rollups.

HOT TIP: Introduce peanut butter, honey and jam at around 12 months of age.

French Toast Treat

1 slice bread (crusts removed)
1 egg yolk
3 tablespoons Karicare Follow-On milk
1 teaspoon margarine

Whisk egg yolk and milk together. Coat bread in mixture. Melt margarine in frypan. Lightly fry bread either side until golden brown. Cut into small triangles and serve.

Cheese Melts

2 tablespoons grated cheese
1 slice bread
1 pinch low-sodium green herb stock (optional)

Sprinkle grated cheese over bread.

MICROWAVE: Cook on HIGH 20-30 seconds until cheese melts.

CONVENTIONAL: Place under griller until cheese bubbles.

BOTH: Sprinkle with green herb stock. Cut into small fingers and serve.

SUGGESTED SNACKS

People often think snacks are bad for children and try to prevent them from eating between meals. But toddlers' energy needs are high and they have a limited capacity for food. So they really need to eat every 3 to 4 hours. Snacks should be offered midway between meals.

The important thing is the timing of snacks and the type of food that is consumed. Ideas for quick but healthy snacks don't always come easily to a busy parent. Don't be tempted to dump a handful of potato chips or a piece of chocolate on the high chair tray to appease a grizzling baby. These have little nutritional value in relationship to the calories they contain. Keep the snacks in this chapter handy in the pantry and serve them as part of the day's regular routine.

Many of the Finger Foods from earlier in this chapter will double as snacks. Check back for more ideas.

REMEMBER: Always check the temperature of cooked food before feeding it to baby. Beware of microwave "hot-spots".

SIMPLE SNACKS :

Simple snacks consist of healthy, easily prepared items such as:

7 months

Carrot or other pieces of raw fruit or vegetables – either whole or grated.

8 months

Sultanas or raisins – steam or stew them to soften which will prevent choking

Cheese – cut it into handy sticks that baby can hold and suck.

Mandarin segments – remove as much white pith as possible. Don't break all the segments apart. Teach baby to do it himself, but stay with him to make sure he doesn't put too large a piece in his mouth.

Fruits – Baby is now old enough to have pieces of raw fruit to hold and suck. Once teeth come through, make sure baby doesn't bite off small pieces and choke. Never leave baby unattended while eating.

Try wedges of apple, pear, peach, plum, apricot, banana, nectarine or melon. Wedges of orange can be given to baby after 8 months – it is too acidic to include earlier.

Home-made Rusks
Commercially prepared rusks are excellent value and conveniently packaged. However, you may wish to make your own.

Just take 2-3 slices of thick toast bread. Cut the bread slices into five thin fingers. Place them on an oven tray. Bake at 100°C for 2 hours until really dry and hard. Leave to cool in the oven, then store in an airtight container.

Bought Biscuits to Suck

Plain Crackers – 2-3 small or 1 large plain cracker biscuits – and that's it!

Plain Yoghurt

4

Getting There

10-12 Months

By ten months to a year, baby usually needs less mashed foods. He will be eating with his fingers and may attempt to use a spoon. Cutting teeth requires tasty items to suck and gnaw at to help get those irritating teeth through tender gums.

Encourage baby to feed himself as much as possible with his own spoon. Let him dip and suck it while you are feeding him. He will soon learn how to eat from it.

Increase baby's participation in feeding by offering him the lead whenever you can. Let him feed himself as soon as he shows the inclination and the ability. These may not appear at the same time so allow for the mess with good-sized bibs and a plastic sheet or layer of newspaper under the high chair.

Baby may be passionately interested in food or only tolerant about eating. He may be curious and willing to experiment or he may dislike the introduction of new foods. He may have a powerful hunger drive or only mild reactions to being hungry. All these are normal responses to eating, so don't panic, and be as supportive as possible.

Encourage baby to drink through a straw. This leads to a variety of delicious delights. It also means not having to pack bottles and drinking cups everywhere you go.

Baby must still be on breast milk or formula as a primary drink. For milk used in recipes, the preferred choice is still breast milk or formula rather than whole cow's milk. Baby should still be avoiding egg white.

REMEMBER: Always check the temperature of cooked food before feeding it to baby. Beware of microwave "hot-spots".

Getting There
Index

Apple Crumble   76

Apricot Smoothie   75

Baked Bean Bonanza   64

Banana Smoothie   75

Beef and Vegetable Casserole   70

Chicken Casserole   70

Chicken in Parsley Sauce   63

Chocolate Fruit Smoothie   76

Creamed Corn Surprise   66

Fish Cake Feast   72

Fruit Rabbit   73

Hash Browns   66

Irish Stew   65

Jelly Belly Delight   74

Liver and Rice   63

Macaroni and Cheese   68

Macaroni Cheese   69

Peach Smoothie   75

Potato Stuffing   68

Rice and Vegetables   65

Salmon Kedgeree   62

Sizzling Sausage   62

Spaghetti Babynaise   71

Strawberry Smoothie   75

Suggested Finger Foods   77

Suggested Snacks   80

Super Sundae   74

Tasty Tuna and Rice   64

Tiny Fish and Chips   73

Tomato Stuffing   67

Salmon Kedgeree

2 tablespoons tinned salmon
$\frac{1}{2}$ cup cooked rice
1 teaspoon finely chopped onion
1 tablespoon finely chopped capsicum
1 teaspoon butter or margarine
1 tablespoon grated cheese

MICROWAVE: Place butter and onion in dish and cook 30 seconds on HIGH. Stir in capsicum and cook a further 20 seconds. Add rice, salmon and cheese. Stir to combine. Cook 1 minute on HIGH. Cool and serve.

CONVENTIONAL: Melt butter in small saucepan. Add onion and capsicum. Cook 1-2 minutes. Add other ingredients and stir to combine. Cook a further 2-3 minutes until cheese is melted, stirring to prevent sticking. Cool and serve.

Sizzling Sausage

1 good quality beef sausage
2 tablespoons grated cheese

Use a sausage that you know won't contain any hard or gristly lumps.

Grill sausage in usual manner until well cooked. Cut in half lengthwise. Sprinkle each half with grated cheese. Place under griller until cheese bubbles. Allow to cool and cut into bite-sized pieces.

Chicken in Parsley Sauce

2 tablespoons cooked and diced chicken
1 teaspoon butter or margarine
2 teaspoon flour
100 ml Karicare Follow-On milk formula
1 teaspoon finely chopped parsley

MICROWAVE: Melt butter in small bowl for 10 seconds on HIGH. Stir in flour. Cook a further 10 seconds, then stir in milk. Cook 1½-2 minutes on HIGH, stirring occasionally, until mixture boils and thickens. Add cooked chicken and parsley. Cook on HIGH 1-2 minutes more until boiling point is again reached. Cool and serve.

Liver and Rice

2 tablespoons cooked lamb's fry, minced or finely chopped
½ cup freshly cooked rice
2 tablespoons creamed sweetcorn

Combine ingredients in bowl or saucepan.

MICROWAVE: Cook on HIGH 1 minute. Cool and serve.

CONVENTIONAL: Gently heat through until boiling. Stir to avoid mixture sticking to bottom of saucepan. Cool and serve.

Tasty Tuna and Rice

2 tablespoons tinned tuna (preferably in spring water)
1 teaspoon mayonnaise
2 tablespoons grated cheese
1 teaspoon finely chopped parsley
$^{1}/_{2}$ cup freshly cooked hot rice

Combine all ingredients in small bowl or saucepan.

MICROWAVE: Cook 30-40 seconds on HIGH, until cheese melts. Cool and serve.

CONVENTIONAL: Stir over low heat until cheese melts. Cool and serve.

Baked Bean Bonanza

$^{1}/_{2}$ cup baked beans
1 tablespoon chopped capsicum
1 tablespoon grated cheese

Combine all ingredients in small bowl or saucepan.

MICROWAVE: Cook 30-40 seconds on HIGH until heated through.

CONVENTIONAL: Stir over heat until heated through.

BOTH: Cool and serve.

HOT TIP: Serve on small fingers of toast if desired and baby will be able to feed himself.

Irish Stew

1 lamb neck chop (or small loin chop)
1 small onion
1 small potato
1 small carrot
1 piece parsnip
2 cups water
1 tablespoon cornflour

Trim any fat from meat. Slice onion. Put onion and meat into saucepan with water. Bring to boil. Simmer 1 hour. Add peeled and diced vegetables. Simmer a further 30 minutes. Combine cornflour with $1/4$ cup of extra water. Return stew to boiling point. Add cornflour mixture and stir until thickened. Cool. Remove meat from bones and cut into bite-sized pieces. Discard bones and any gristle. Mash with a fork if needed.

Rice and Vegetables

$1/2$ cup freshly cooked rice
3-4 freshly cooked vegetables (possibly from your own dinner)
2 tablespoons grated cheese

Combine all ingredients. The heat from freshly cooked rice and vegetables will melt cheese. Cool and serve.

Creamed Corn Surprise

$1/2$ cup creamed sweetcorn
1 tablespoon finely chopped capsicum

Combine ingredients in bowl or saucepan.

MICROWAVE: Cook on HIGH 1 minute until mixture boils, stirring once.

CONVENTIONAL: Stir over heat until boiling. Cool and serve.

Hash Browns

1 medium potato (peeled and grated)
1 egg yolk
2 teaspoons oil

Mix together grated potato and egg yolk. Heat oil in a small frypan. Place tablespoons of potato mixture in pan. Flatten with back of spoon. Fry on each side for a few minutes until potato is cooked and golden brown.

BABY BONUS: Makes three hash brown potato cakes.

HOT TIP: Serve as a meal on their own or as an accompaniment to meat, fish or chicken.

Tomato Stuffing

1 large tomato
1 teaspoon finely chopped onion
1 tablespoon grated cheese
1 pinch mixed herbs

Cut top off tomato, taking care to remove any tough stalk. Scoop out tomato pips and flesh into a small bowl or saucepan. Mix tomato pulp with other ingredients.

MICROWAVE: Cook 1½ minutes on HIGH.

CONVENTIONAL: Bring tomato, onion and herbs to the boil, then simmer until pulp is very soft. Remove from heat and stir in cheese.

BOTH: Allow to cool before serving. Remember melted cheese gets very hot.

HOT TIP: Older children can have stuffing returned to tomato shell, but cooked tomato skin is generally disliked by babies and toddlers. Serve them the stuffing in a small dish.

Potato Stuffing

1 medium potato
1 teaspoon finely chopped onion
1 tablespoon grated cheese
2 teaspoons Karicare Follow-On milk formula
1 pinch low-sodium green herb stock

Prick potato several times with a fork.

MICROWAVE: Place potato on small plate. Cook on HIGH 3-4 minutes, turning over once. Allow to cool slightly. Scoop out cooked potato into a small bowl. Mix in other ingredients. Return mixture to plate and re-heat 40 seconds on HIGH. Cool before serving.

CONVENTIONAL: Bake potato 30-40 minutes in moderate oven until soft. Allow to cool slightly. Scoop out cooked potato into a small bowl. Mix in other ingredients. Place mixture in dish and re-heat under griller. Cool before serving.

HOT TIP: Older children can have stuffing returned to potato shell, but potato skins are generally too fibrous for babies and toddlers. Serve them the stuffing in a small dish.

Macaroni and Cheese

$1/2$ cup cooked macaroni (elbows, shells, spirals etc.)
2 tablespoons grated cheese

Sprinkle cheese over freshly cooked hot macaroni. Cheese will melt.

Macaroni Cheese

$^1/_2$ cup cooked macaroni
1 teaspoon butter or margarine
1 teaspoon flour
100 ml Karicare Follow-On milk formula
2 tablespoons grated cheese

MICROWAVE: In small bowl or jug, melt butter 10 seconds on
HIGH. Stir in flour and cook a further 10 seconds. Add milk.
Cook $1^1/_2$-2 minutes, stirring to prevent lumps. Stir in cheese
until melted. Stir in macaroni. Cook 1-2 minutes on HIGH
until boiling. Cool and serve.

CONVENTIONAL: Melt butter in a small saucepan. Stir in
flour and cook a few seconds. Add milk carefully to avoid
lumps. Bring to boil, but don't allow to boil over. Add cheese
and macaroni. Bring back to the boil. Cool and serve.

Beef and Vegetable Casserole

$1/2$ cup finely diced rump steak
2 teaspoons flour
1 tablespoon finely chopped onion
1 small kumara (or sweet potato)
1 small carrot (or $1/2$ large)
1 teaspoon soy sauce
$1/2$ cup water

Toss steak in flour until well coated. Peel and dice vegetables. Combine ingredients in ovenproof dish. Cook at 180°C for 1 hour, until steak is tender. Allow to cool. Mash with a fork or potato masher before serving.

Chicken Casserole

1 small piece chicken (thigh or breast piece is best)
2 teaspoons flour
$1/2$ cup water
1 tablespoon finely chopped onion
1 tablespoon diced capsicum
2 tablespoons creamed sweetcorn
2 tablespoons frozen mixed vegetables

Remove skin and fat from chicken. Toss in flour until well coated. Place in small ovenproof casserole dish with other ingredients. Bake at 180°C for 1 hour. Allow to cool. Remove meat from bones and dice finely. Discard bones and any gristle. Serve.

Spaghetti Babynaise

$^1\!/_2$ cup good quality minced beef
1 tablespoon finely chopped onion
1 tablespoon tomato sauce
2 tablespoons water
1 pinch thyme
$^1\!/_2$ cup cooked spaghetti

MICROWAVE: In a small bowl or jug, cook mince and onion on HIGH 2 minutes until browned, stirring once or twice for even cooking. Add remaining ingredients (except spaghetti) and cook a further 3 minutes. Mash with fork if necessary to separate lumps.

CONVENTIONAL: Combine all ingredients except spaghetti in saucepan. Simmer 10 minutes, stirring often.

BOTH: Chop cooked spaghetti into bite-sized pieces. Spoon meat sauce over noodles and serve.

HOT TIP: Sprinkle with Parmesan cheese if desired.

Fish Cake Feast

Keep a packet of commercially prepared fish cakes handy in the freezer – quick and easy to prepare.

    1 frozen fish cake
    a selection of baby's favourite raw vegetables

MICROWAVE: Put fish cake on a plate and cook on HIGH for 20-30 seconds each side.

CONVENTIONAL: Grill 2 minutes each side.

BOTH: Place fish cake in centre of plate. Cut into 6 wedges. Surround with carrot sticks, tomato slices, capsicum rings, bean sprouts, etc. and serve.

Tiny Fish and Chips

Deep-fried food can be too fatty for baby's digestive system. This recipe contains less fat than take-away fish and chips.

1 fish cake or 2 fish fingers
8-10 commercially packaged frozen chips

Place fish cake and chips on plate or grilling tray.

MICROWAVE: Cook 1 minute on HIGH. Turn fish cake over and stir chips. Cook on HIGH a further minute.

CONVENTIONAL: Grill 5-6 minutes. Turn fish cake over and stir chips. Grill a further 4-5 minutes. Add a little tomato sauce if desired.

Fruit Rabbit

$\frac{1}{2}$ banana
1 glace cherry
a small handful raisins/sultanas

Cut two round slices from banana for eyes. Slice other piece lengthwise for two pointy ears. Cherry is for nose. Sultanas can be shaped into a smiling mouth. Two sultanas of similar size and shape can be used for centres of eyes on top of banana rings.

BABY BONUS: Other food can be substituted to suit. Sliced apple or orange segment for mouth, kiwifruit circles for eyes marshmallow for nose. Use leftovers in a fruit salad for the rest of the family if desired.

Jelly Belly Delight

1 serving fruit salad
50 ml fruit juice (or Ribena)
2 teaspoons gelatine
2 tablespoons boiling water

Stir gelatine in boiling water until dissolved. Mix with fruit salad and fruit juice. Pour into jelly mould and leave to set.

Super Sundae

1 scoop ice cream
2 teaspoons Milo
2 teaspoons boiling water
1 pink party wafer

Dissolve Milo in boiling water and allow to cool. Place scoop of ice cream in a small serving dish. Pour cooled Milo over ice cream. Press one edge of wafer into sundae. Serve immediately.

HOT TIP: Be creative. Cut wafer in half diagonally and position it as sails on top of ice cream. Or break it into odd-shaped pieces and press into sundae. Try strips or diamond shapes for variety.

Banana Smoothie

Smoothies are not drinks for a baby. They are so filling, they make a complete meal or dessert.

  $1/2$ small banana
  $1/2$ cup Karicare Follow-On milk formula
  1 small scoop plain ice cream

Blend all ingredients together in kitchen whizz, blender or with egg beater. Serve immediately in a tall tumbler with a straw.

HOT TIP: Avoid serving the small lumps of fruit in the bottom of the whizz, as they may block the straw.

Strawberry Smoothie

Replace banana with 2-3 large strawberries when in season.

HOT TIP: Strawberries can cause an allergic reaction. If you have a family history of allergies, it is best to leave strawberries until baby is over 12 months old.

Peach Smoothie

Replace banana with $1/4$ cup tinned peaches in juice – no sugar added.

Apricot Smoothie

Replace banana with $1/4$ cup tinned apricots in juice – no sugar added.

Chocolate Fruit Smoothie

Substitute chocolate ice cream in all previous recipes.

Apple Crumble

$^{1}/_{2}$ cup stewed apples
Topping:
2 teaspoons margarine
3 tablespoons rolled oats
1 tablespoon shredded coconut
1 teaspoon brown sugar

MICROWAVE: Melt margarine in small bowl for 20 seconds on HIGH. Stir in rolled oats, coconut and brown sugar. Spoon apples into base of another dish. Spread topping over apple and pat down gently with the back of a spoon. Cook 1 minute on HIGH. Allow to cool.

CONVENTIONAL: Melt margarine in small saucepan. Stir in rolled oats, coconut and brown sugar. Spoon stewed apple into bottom of a small ovenproof dish. Spread topping over apple and pat down gently with the back of a spoon. Bake 10-15 minutes in a moderate oven.

SUGGESTED FINGER FOODS

Raw Fruit Platter

By 10-12 months, baby can manage raw fruit on a platter.

Try an assortment of peach slices, pineapple chunks, pear sticks, apple slices, banana rings, watermelon chunks, pawpaw fingers, orange segments, strawberry halves, avocado slices, mandarin segments, kiwifruit slices, rock melon wedges or grapes and plums (quartered and pipped).

It probably won't make much difference to baby, but you might enjoy being a little artistic and arranging the fruit in a pattern – maybe a face or an animal . . .

HOT TIP: Add one or two marshmallows as an extra treat.

BABY BONUS: Rather than wasting the remaining halves of fruit, the rest of the family might also enjoy a fruit platter.

Raw Vegetable Platter

Baby can now manage raw vegetables as well. Try cauliflower florets, carrot sticks, cucumber circles, tomato wedges, raw beans, capsicum rings (crisp, cold and delicious), bean sprouts, courgette rings, cabbage stalks or celery sticks (de-stringed). Once again, take a little time to arrange food in an attractive pattern. Baby will love to pick and choose from the selection.

Fruit Kebab

An interesting change from a fruit platter . . .

    slices or cubes of various fruit
    1 marshmallow
    1 bamboo skewer

Thread fruit onto skewer and top with marshmallow. Cut sharp tip off skewer in case baby scratches himself. Take skewer away as soon as baby has removed all the fruit.

BABY BONUS: As with the Fruit Platter, the rest of the family may like to try fruit kebabs using any remaining fruit.

Vegetable Kebab

An interesting change from a vegetable platter . . .

Thread vegetables in an interesting and colourful sequence on skewer. Cut sharp tip off skewer in case baby scratches himself. Take skewer away as soon as baby has removed all the vegetables.

HOT TIP: Small pieces of cold meat (chicken, ham, beef, salami, sausage etc.) can be alternated with vegetables.

Sandwich Shapes

2 slices bread
margarine or butter
desired filling – Marmite, mashed baked beans, cheese spread,
    spaghetti, luncheon meat, mashed banana etc.

Make sandwich as normal, cutting off crusts. Cut into interesting
shapes with small cookie cutters. The leftover trimmings make
interesting shapes too, so serve them as well.

HOT TIP: Introduce honey, peanut butter and jam after 12
months.

Ice cream in a cone

*This is a bit messy at first but, with a little practice, baby will soon
get the hang of it.*

1 plain ice cream cone
1 small scoop ice cream
    (any flavour, but not ones containing nuts)

HOT TIP: The occasional serving of ice cream will not harm
baby. Just remember to have it as a treat and not as an everyday
food.

Plus all previous Finger Food recipes.

SUGGESTED SNACKS

Cheesy Crackers

2-3 small plain crackers
2-3 small thin slices of cheese

Cover each cracker with a piece of cheese. Place on serving plate or grilling tray.

MICROWAVE: Cook 15-20 seconds on HIGH until cheese bubbles.

CONVENTIONAL: Place under griller until cheese melts.

BOTH: Allow to cool. Remember melted cheese gets very hot.

Cheesy Biscuits

1 cup self-raising flour
2 teaspoons icing sugar
1 pinch salt
2 tablespoons butter or margarine
3 tablespoons grated cheese
milk to mix

Combine dry ingredients. Rub in butter. Add grated cheese and enough milk to mix to a firm dough. Knead on floured board. Roll out as thinly as possible. Cut into fingers and place around edges of microwave turn-table or on baking tray. Prick several times with a fork.

MICROWAVE: Cook in two batches of 10 on HIGH for 2 minutes.

CONVENTIONAL: Bake 10 minutes at 200°C.

BOTH: Store in airtight container. Makes 20.

HOT TIP: Most biscuits are best cooked in the oven. If you are in a hurry, microwave baking is perfectly acceptable, just a little different in colour and texture.

Golden Baby Biscuits

$^{1}/_{3}$ cup flour
2 tablespoons coconut
$^{1}/_{2}$ cup Robinsons Muesli
2 tablespoons butter or margarine
1 tablespoon golden syrup
2 tablespoons milk

Mix together flour, coconut and Robinsons Muesli. Melt butter and golden syrup in milk. Stir into dry ingredients. Place in small teaspoonfuls around edge of microwave turn-table or on baking tray. Flatten with a fork.

MICROWAVE: Cook in 2 batches of 12 on MEDIUM for 1$^{1}/_{2}$ minutes.

CONVENTIONAL: Bake 10-12 minutes at 180°C.

BOTH: Store in an airtight container. Makes 24 small biscuits.

HOT TIP: As with *Cheesy Biscuits*, these are best cooked in the oven but microwave baking is fine for those in a hurry.

Delicious Crusts

1 thick crust from end of loaf
selected topping(s) –
   Vegemite – alone or with grated cheese, pate – alone or with
   tomato relish, cottage cheese – alone or with low-sodium
   green herb stock, spaghetti – alone or with cream cheese,
   tomato relish – alone or with cheese spread . . . plus tasty
   combinations of the above.

Crusts from the ends of your loaf of bread are ideal for baby to
suck when annoying teeth are trying to come through. Use nice
thick crusts, spread with butter (if desired) and/or chosen
topping. Cut into long thin strips – at least four strips per crust.
Give to baby one at a time.

Mousetraps

4 slices bread, crusts removed
$^1/_4$ cup grated cheese
1 tablespoon melted butter
Vegemite

Spread lightly with Vegemite. Combine melted butter with
grated cheese and spread this over Vegemite. Cut each slice of
bread into 3 fingers. Place on cold baking tray. Bake in a slow
oven (100°C) 1 hour. Cool. Store in an airtight container. Makes
12 mousetraps.

5

Graduation

Over 12 Months

At twelve months, baby can eat many of the same things as the rest of the family. However, he may eat at different times, and will still require food to be cut into small pieces.

Present meals in a form that is easily managed. Support his efforts to use a spoon by himself. Helping him because you can do it faster (and cleaner) stifles his initiative and opportunity to learn. Keep meal times enjoyable. Talk to him in a quiet and encouraging manner while he eats. Don't overwhelm him with attention, but keep him company. Above all, don't put an unreasonable amount of time into preparing a meal, only to be disappointed if it is not all eaten.

Toddlers are allowed their likes and dislikes. If your toddler shows a marked dislike for any food, don't force the issue. There are plenty of alternatives in this book. Try the disliked food again in a few months, or disguise it in a casserole. If that doesn't work, leave well alone.

Most recipes in this section can be prepared for the whole family if amounts are increased. Baby can now have cow's milk rather than Follow-On milk formula. However, Follow-On formula can be used up until 2 years of age if desired, especially if baby isn't eating a wide variety of foods. Follow-On formula provides a good source of necessary vitamins and minerals for older babies up to 24 months.

Egg white, shellfish and pork can now be safely incorporated into baby's diet.

REMEMBER: Always check the temperature of cooked food before feeding it to baby. Beware of microwave "hot-spots".

Graduation
Index

Advanced Creamy Egg Custard	101
Baked Custard	104
Boiled Egg and Soldiers	89
Bread and Butter Pudding	103
Cheese Omelette	89
Chocolate Goo	101
Coddled Egg	88
Egg Foo Yong	91
Egg in a Dish	91
Fishburger Treat	96
Flummery	110
Fruit Fritters	100
Funny Face Eggs	92
Hamburger Heaven	96
Icy Slicy	107
Kitchen Hangi	97
Little Fruit Pudding	107
Macaroni Custard	106
Meat and Onion Fritters	100
Mini Hot Dog	97

Mini Meat Kebabs	95
Omelette on Toast	90
Pancakes	108
Peanut Dip	94
Petite Pikelets	109
Pita Pocket	98
Rice Pudding	105
Savoury Egg Supreme	92
Savoury Pancakes	108
Scrambled Egg	88
Seafood Fritters	100
Semolina and Egg Custard	102
Semolina Supreme	102
Stuffed Sausage Supreme	94
Suggested Snacks	111
Sweetcorn Omelette	90
Tuna Pie	93
Vegetable Fritters	99
Vegies and Dip	95

Scrambled Egg

1 egg
50 ml milk
$^1/_2$ teaspoon low-sodium green herb stock

Whisk egg and milk together in a small bowl.

MICROWAVE: Cook on HIGH 1 minute. Stir and add herb stock. Cook a further 30 seconds.

CONVENTIONAL: Cook in a small non-stick frypan (or ordinary pan with a little butter to prevent sticking). When nearly set, sprinkle with stock.

BOTH: Stir once again and allow to cool before serving.

Coddled Egg

1 egg
saucepan boiling water

Ease egg into boiling water taking care it doesn't burst. Allow to boil one minute. Remove pan from heat. Let egg stand in hot water for 7-8 minutes. The white will be soft and easier for baby to digest.

Boiled Egg and Soldiers

1 egg
1 slice soft white bread, buttered or unbuttered

Bring saucepan of water to the boil. Gently ease raw egg into water, taking care it doesn't crack. Boil 3 minutes for a runny yolk. Allow to cool.

To Serve: Cut top off egg. Dip soldiers in egg yolk and pass to baby to eat. Spoon feed remainder of egg.

Cheese Omelette

1 egg
2 tablespoons milk
1 tablespoon grated cheese
1 teaspoon butter or margarine

Whisk egg and milk together. Melt butter in small frying pan. (Use non-stick frypan if available). Pour in egg mixture. With fish slice, draw cooked mixture from around edge of pan towards centre, until all is lightly cooked and set. Sprinkle with cheese. Fold one half of omelette over onto the other half. Remove from heat. Cool and serve.

Omelette on Toast

1 egg
4 tablespoons milk
$\frac{1}{4}$ teaspoon low-sodium green herb stock
1 slice bread

Toast bread. Butter if desired. Whisk egg and milk together.

MICROWAVE: Cook on HIGH 1 minute. Stir. Sprinkle with green herb stock and cook a further 30 seconds or until set.

CONVENTIONAL: Cook egg mixture in non-stick frypan until set. Sprinkle with stock.

BOTH: Spoon mixture on toast, pressing it down gently. Cut toast in half and then into 4 or 5 fingers. This makes it easier for baby to pick up. If he likes it, he'll manage to eat it.

Sweetcorn Omelette

1 egg
4 tablespoons milk
2 tablespoons creamed sweetcorn

Whisk egg and milk together in a small bowl.

MICROWAVE: Cook on HIGH 1 minute. Stir in sweetcorn. Cook a further 30-40 seconds or until set. Cool and serve.

CONVENTIONAL: Cook egg mixture in non-stick frypan until just set. Add sweetcorn and spread over one half of omelette. Fold one half of omelette over other. Cook a further minute to warm corn through. Cool and serve.

Egg Foo Yong

1 egg
4 tablespoons milk
1 teaspoon finely chopped onion
2 tablespoons frozen mixed vegetables (thawed)
$1/2$ teaspoon soy sauce
1 teaspoon butter or oil

Whisk together egg and milk.

MICROWAVE: Place butter, onion and mixed vegetables in bowl and cook on HIGH 1 minute. Stir in egg mixture. Cook on HIGH 1 minute. Stir. Cook a further 30-40 seconds until set.

CONVENTIONAL: Melt butter in small frypan. Lightly cook onion and mixed vegetables 1 minute. Add egg mixture. Cook by drawing cooked edges into centre until all is set. Flip cooked mixture over to brown other side.

BOTH: Drizzle with soy sauce. Cool and serve.

Egg in a Dish

For microwave only.

1 egg
1 tablespoon milk

Crack egg into small dish or cup. Pierce yolk 2-3 times with a sharp pointed knife. Spoon milk over yolk (this helps with cooking). Cover dish with gladwrap. Cook on MEDIUM 50-60 seconds until just set. Let stand 1 minute before serving.

Savoury Egg Supreme

1 hard-boiled egg
$^1/_2$ teaspoon mayonnaise or salad dressing
$^1/_2$ teaspoon finely chopped parsley

Chop egg into small pieces and mash with a fork. Stir in mayonnaise and parsley. Serve.

Funny Face Eggs

A novel way to serve boiled eggs.

1 egg
water to cover

Draw a funny face on egg shell with pencil. Perhaps round eyes with long eyelashes, curly hair, big ears, smiling mouth and a bow tie. Boil egg in usual manner – hard or soft according to baby's tastes.

BABY BONUS: *Funny Face Eggs* are popular for a lifetime. When children are old enough, let them do their own drawing.

Tuna Pie

2 tablespoons canned tuna (preferably in water)
1 teaspoon butter or margarine
2 teaspoons flour
100 ml milk
1 teaspoon finely chopped parsley
$^1/_2$ hard-boiled egg
2 tablespoons frozen peas (thawed)
1 cup freshly cooked mashed potatoes

MICROWAVE: Melt butter in small casserole dish – 10 seconds on HIGH. Stir in flour and cook a further 10 seconds. Stir in milk. Cook 1$^1/_2$-2 minutes on HIGH, stirring occasionally, until mixture boils and thickens. Add flaked tuna and parsley. Slice egg and place in a layer over fish. Spread a layer of peas over eggs and finally a layer of mashed potatoes. Cook on MEDIUM HIGH 5 minutes. Cool and serve.

CONVENTIONAL: Melt butter in a small saucepan. Stir in flour and cook a few seconds. Add milk carefully to avoid lumps. Bring to boil, but don't allow to boil over. Add parsley and flaked tuna. Spread mixture into base of a small casserole dish. Slice egg and place in a layer over fish. Spread a layer of peas over eggs and lastly a layer of mashed potatoes. Bake at 180°C for 15-20 minutes. Cool and serve.

Stuffed Sausage Supreme

1 cooked sausage (grilled, boiled, microwaved)
$1/4$ cup mashed potatoes
2 tablespoons cooked peas
2 tablespoons grated cheese

Cut sausage in half lengthwise, but not all the way through so that both halves are "hinged". Mix peas in with potatoes and stuff sausage with mixture. Sprinkle with grated cheese.

MICROWAVE: Place stuffed sausage on small serving plate and cook on HIGH 50-60 seconds until cheese melts.

CONVENTIONAL: Place under griller 1-2 minutes until cheese melts.

BOTH: Cut into bite-sized pieces.

Peanut Dip

A useful accompaniment to mini kebabs, potato wedges, vegetable platters etc.

2 tablespoons peanut butter
4 tablespoons milk
1 teaspoon soy sauce

MICROWAVE: Cook ingredients on MEDIUM 1 minute, stirring once or twice until smooth.

CONVENTIONAL: Cook over low heat, stirring constantly until combined.

BOTH: Serve with fingers of pita bread or thick crusts.

Vegies and Dip

platter vegetables
(raw or par-boiled if baby hasn't many teeth)
Peanut Dip (from previous recipe)

Suggested vegetables – raw carrot sticks, cauliflower florets, celery sticks, capsicum strips, zucchini sticks, cabbage stalks. Par-boiled Brussels sprout halves or potato, kumara, parsnip and turnip sticks.

Show baby how to dip and eat.

HOT TIP: Include cheese sticks for further variety.

Mini Meat Kebabs

small piece rump steak (around 100 grams)
1 tablespoon soy sauce
2 bamboo skewers

Cut steak into small cubes. Marinate in soy sauce in fridge for 30 minutes. Thread steak onto bamboo skewers. Grill 10 minutes, turning frequently to prevent burning. Remove meat from skewers before serving. Serve with *Peanut Dip* from previous recipe.

Hamburger Heaven

1 small bread roll or old English muffin
2 tablespoons mince
1 thin slice cheese
1 slice tomato
1 slice beetroot
tomato sauce to taste

Fill hamburger with food your baby likes. Cut roll or muffin in half. Lightly toast both sides under griller. Butter if desired. Cover one half with meat pattie, tomato sauce, cheese, tomato, etc. Top with other half. Serve without cutting. Baby will take it apart and eat his favourite bits first.

To Make and Cook Meat Pattie
Press mince into a flat circle. (No need to bother with onion, herbs, spices etc. at this age).

MICROWAVE: Place pattie on small plate. Cook on HIGH 30 seconds. Press down firmly with back of spoon, then turn over. Cook a further 20 seconds on HIGH.

CONVENTIONAL: Fry in a non-stick frypan 2-3 minutes each side until juices run clear. Flatten with fish slice as it cooks.

Fishburger Treat

Substitute a cooked fish cake for the meat pattie in the previous recipe.

Kitchen Hangi

1 small piece chicken
1 small pork chop or pork slice
1 small kumara or sweet potato
1 small piece pumpkin
5 leaves silverbeet
2 cups water

Wash silverbeet and cut off any long stalks. Wrap each item of food in a leaf of silverbeet and place it in a lidded casserole dish. Add water and cover. Bake 2 hours at 150°C. Long, slow cooking gives the taste of a real hangi. Throw away all silverbeet as it turns black and tasteless. Meat should be tender enough to fall off the bone. Discard bones and fat.

Mini Hot Dog

1 small oval roll (a Holland roll is ideal)
1 Cheerio
1 tablespoon grated cheese
tomato sauce to taste

Heat Cheerio in microwave or boiling water. Split open roll and insert Cheerio. Add tomato sauce and sprinkle with cheese.

MICROWAVE: Cook on serving plate 20-30 seconds until cheese melts.

CONVENTIONAL: Place under griller to melt cheese.

BOTH: Serve whole. Baby will take it apart and eat it in his own preferred order.

Pita Pocket

3 tablespoons canned tuna (preferably in water)
1 small finely chopped spring onion
1 teaspoon finely chopped parsley
1 tablespoon mayonnaise
2 tablespoons grated cheese
1 small round of pita bread

Mix all ingredients (except pita bread) together in small bowl or saucepan.

MICROWAVE: Cook on HIGH 40-50 seconds. Stir. Cook 20 seconds longer.

CONVENTIONAL: Heat gently until cheese melts.

BOTH: Cut bread in half. Open pocket and fill with fish mixture. Return to microwave or place under griller briefly to heat through. Cut into small wedge-shaped pieces.
Baby Bonus: Makes 2 stuffed pita pockets.

Vegetable Fritters

⅓ cup flour (standard or self-raising)
1 egg
pinch salt
¼ cup grated cheese
1 teaspoon finely chopped parsley (optional)
¼ cup grated vegetable of choice – e.g. zucchini, pumpkins,
     kumara, potato, carrot, or creamed-style sweetcorn.
milk to mix
50/50 combination of oil and butter or margarine to cook

Mix all ingredients together to form a stiff batter. Heat oil and butter in a frypan. Drop tablespoon of mixture into oil/butter. Cook one side until batter is peppered with several air holes. Turn over and cook other side until golden brown. Drain and cool on a paper towel before serving.

HOT TIP: For variety and a little fun, cook fritters in different sizes and shapes. Perhaps one quite large and one very small. Maybe a cat or teddy bear shape, or a long oval. Even several small circles together to form a caterpillar.

Fruit Fritters

Remove cheese and parsley from the previous recipe. Replace grated vegetables with one of the following fruit suggestions – mashed banana, grated apple, unsweetened crushed pineapple, tinned peaches or apricots in juice – not sugar.

Seafood Fritters

Replace cheese in *Vegetable Fritters* with a small chopped onion. Replace vegetables with minced cooked mussels, cockles or pipis.

Meat and Onion Fritters

Add 1 small chopped onion to *Vegetable Fritters* recipe. Replace vegetables in recipe with finely diced cold meat, ham, corned beef, roast lamb, chicken, beef etc.

Advanced Creamy Egg Custard

150 ml milk
1 egg
2 teaspoons cornflour
1 teaspoon sugar

Whisk all ingredients together in a small bowl or saucepan.

MICROWAVE: Cook on MEDIUM 2-3 minutes stirring every minute. Do not boil.

CONVENTIONAL: Stir in saucepan over low heat until thickened. Do not allow to boil.

BABY BONUS: Actually makes a pleasant custard for the whole family. Recipe can be doubled without difficulty.

Chocolate Goo

150 ml milk
1 egg
2 teaspoons cornflour
1 teaspoon baking cocoa
2 teaspoons sugar

Whisk all ingredients together in a small bowl or saucepan.

MICROWAVE: Cook 2-3 minutes on MEDIUM, stirring 2-3 times. Do not boil.

CONVENTIONAL: Stir in saucepan over low heat until thickened. Do not allow to boil.

Semolina and Egg Custard

75 ml milk
1 egg
$^1/_2$ teaspoon sugar
$^1/_2$ quantity of cooked semolina (see *Semolina Pudding* recipe,
Chapter 2 page 28)

Whisk egg and milk together in a small bowl or saucepan.

MICROWAVE: Cook 1 minute on MEDIUM. Stir. Cook a
further minute, stirring twice more to ensure even cooking. Do
not boil.

CONVENTIONAL: Stir over low heat until thickened. Do not
boil.

BOTH: Combine custard with cooked semolina. Allow to cool.

Semolina Supreme

1 quantity of *Semolina and Egg Custard* (from previous recipe)
$^1/_2$ ripe banana

Thoroughly mash banana and add to custard mixture.

Bread and Butter Pudding

2 slices buttered bread (crusts removed)
2 teaspoons jam
handful of sultanas
1 egg
$^1/_2$ cup milk
1 teaspoon sugar
2 drops of vanilla essence

Spread jam over bread. Cut into 1 inch squares. Place in bottom of small dish. Sprinkle with sultanas. Whisk together egg, milk, sugar and essence. Pour over bread.

MICROWAVE: Cook 3-4 minutes on MEDIUM. Halfway through, gently draw cooked outer edges into centre to help with even cooking.

CONVENTIONAL: Bake at 180°C for 25-30 minutes until custard is set and top is browned.

BABY BONUS: Makes enough for two – perhaps it could be shared with another family member as it cannot be frozen.

Baked Custard

½ cup milk
1 egg
1 teaspoon sugar
2-3 drops vanilla essence
sprinkle of nutmeg (if desired)

MICROWAVE: Cook milk 1 minute on HIGH until tiny bubbles appear around edge. Do not allow to boil. Whisk egg, sugar and essence together in small bowl. Beat in hot milk. Sprinkle with nutmeg if desired. Cook on MEDIUM LOW 2-2½ minutes until set.

CONVENTIONAL: Heat milk in saucepan until tiny bubbles appear around edge. Do not allow to boil. Whisk egg, sugar and essence together in a small dish. Beat in hot milk. Sprinkle with nutmeg if desired. Place dish in a shallow tray of water. Bake 1 hour at 150°C or until custard is set.

Rice Pudding

$^1\!/_2$ cup milk
1 egg
1 teaspoon sugar
2-3 drops vanilla essence
$^1\!/_2$ cup freshly cooked and drained rice
sprinkle of nutmeg (if desired)

MICROWAVE: Cook milk 1 minute on HIGH until tiny bubbles appear around edge. Do not allow to boil. Whisk egg, sugar and essence together in a small microwave-safe bowl. Beat in hot milk. Stir in hot rice. Sprinkle with nutmeg if desired. Cook on MEDIUM LOW 2 minutes. Stir by drawing cooked edges into centre. Cook a further 20 seconds.

CONVENTIONAL: Heat milk in saucepan until tiny bubbles appear around edge. Do not allow to boil. Whisk egg, sugar and essence together in a dish. Beat in hot milk. Stir in cooked rice. Sprinkle with nutmeg if desired. Place dish in a shallow tray of water. Bake 1 hour at 150°C or until custard is set.

BOTH: Cool and serve.

Macaroni Custard

$^1/_2$ cup milk
1 egg
1 teaspoon sugar
2-3 drops vanilla essence
$^1/_2$ cup freshly cooked and drained macaroni
sprinkle of nutmeg (if desired)

MICROWAVE: Heat milk in microwave 1 minute on HIGH until tiny bubbles appear around edge. Do not allow to boil. Whisk egg, sugar and essence together in a small microwave-safe bowl. Beat in hot milk. Stir in hot macaroni. Sprinkle with nutmeg if desired. Cook on MEDIUM LOW 2 minutes. Stir by drawing cooked edges into centre. Cook a further 20 seconds.

CONVENTIONAL: Heat milk in saucepan until tiny bubbles appear around edge. Do not allow to boil. Whisk egg, sugar and essence together in a small ovenproof dish. Beat in hot milk. Stir in cooked macaroni. Sprinkle with nutmeg if desired. Place dish in a shallow tray of water. Bake 1 hour at 150°C or until custard is set.

BOTH: Cool and serve.

Icy Slicy

1 small slice ice cream
2 pink party wafers

Sandwich ice cream between wafers and serve.

HOT TIP: If ice cream is in a large container and cannot be sliced easily, scoop it out and press it gently over one wafer before topping with other wafer.

Little Fruit Pudding

25 g butter or margarine
1 tablespoon sugar
1 egg
$^1/_2$ cup self raising flour
1 teaspoon cocoa
$^1/_4$ cup mixed fruit or sultanas
$^1/_4$ cup milk

Cream butter and sugar. Beat in egg. Add dry ingredients and sultanas. Mix to a batter with milk. Spoon into a small lightly greased metal basin. Steam pudding according to usual method for 40-45 minutes.

HOT TIP: Serve with *Advanced Creamy Egg Custard* (this chapter, page 101).

BABY BONUS: Makes enough for 2 meals, but can be readily frozen if necessary.

Pancakes

¹/₂ cup self-raising flour
1 egg
1 tablespoon sugar
1 pinch salt
milk to mix
50/50 mix butter and oil to fry

Combine all ingredients into a smooth pourable batter. Heat butter and oil in small omelette pan. Pour in sufficient mixture to cover bottom of frypan. Allow to cook until several air holes appear in surface of pancake. Flip over and cook other side until golden brown.

BABY BONUS: Makes 2-3 medium-sized pancakes.

HOT TIP: Serve rolled up either plain or, for a special treat, try a topping of golden syrup, lemon juice and brown sugar, fruit puree, honey or jam.

Savoury Pancakes

Omit sugar from previous recipe, and top with one of the following savoury ideas . . . cheese spread, pate, spaghetti, mashed baked beans, *Chicken in Parsley sauce* (Chapter 4, page 63), salmon or tuna.

Petite Pikelets

$^1/_2$ cup self-raising flour
1 egg
1 tablespoon sugar
1 pinch salt
milk to mix
50/50 mix butter and oil to fry

Combine ingredients into a stiff batter. Heat oil and butter in a large heavy-bottomed frypan or griddle. Drop teaspoons into frypan. Cook until several air holes appear in surfaces of pikelets. Flip over and cook other sides until golden brown.

Serve warm with butter, on their own or with a little jam.

HOT TIP: Be creative. Cook pikelets in different shapes. Maybe a cat or teddy bear shape, or a long oval. Even several small circles together to form a caterpillar.

Flummery

This has to be made for the whole family as ingredients cannot be reduced to a single serving.

250 ml unsweetened evaporated milk
1 85 g packet jelly crystals (any flavour)
1 cup boiling water

Chill milk for an hour or so before using. Make up jelly with water and put in fridge until half set. Pour milk into large bowl. Whip with egg beater until light and fluffy. Pour in jelly gradually while beating, until well blended. Return to fridge to set.

BABY BONUS: Either serve baby a portion from the family dish, or pour some into a separate small bowl to set.

HOT TIP: When set, decorate top with a selection of baby's favourite raw fruit.

SUGGESTED SNACKS

All finger foods suggested to date can continue to be served.

Baby is probably eating most meals with his fingers anyway.

Crumpet Bites

Commercially prepared crumpets make a quick and easy finger food meal or snack. Keep a pack of frozen "free-flow" for convenience.

    1 round or oblong crumpet
    1 teaspoon honey or Vegemite
    margarine or butter if desired

MICROWAVE: Heat frozen crumpet on serving plate 30 seconds on HIGH (20 seconds if crumpet fresh).

CONVENTIONAL: Grill 1 or 2 minutes each side to heat through.

BOTH: Spread with butter and honey (or Vegemite). Cut into bite-sized pieces and serve.

Senior Rollups

2 slices bread – crusts removed
butter or margarine
gherkin stick or par-boiled carrot stick
2 tablespoons grated cheese
filling – Vegemite, pate, slice of ham, spaghetti, mashed baked
    beans, tomato relish, shredded lettuce, mashed egg

Butter bread, spreading a little extra butter along one edge of one piece. Overlap slices along this edge, sticking bread together to make a double-sized oblong piece of buttered bread.

Spread with a suitable combination of fillings, such as pate and shredded lettuce, or ham and tomato relish, or simply mashed baked beans. Sprinkle with grated cheese. Place gherkin stick or carrot stick along one short edge. Roll up bread into a tight roll. Place in freezer for 5 minutes to chill and set in shape. Cut roll in half crosswise and then into quarters to make four large pinwheel-shaped rollups.

Stuffed Savoury Egg

1 hard-boiled egg
$^3/_4$ teaspoon mayonnaise or $^1/_2$ teaspoon milk
$^1/_2$ teaspoon finely chopped parsley
1 pinch curry powder

Cut egg in half lengthwise and remove yolk. Mash yolk with mayonnaise, parsley and curry powder. Spoon yolk mixture back into egg white. Serve.

Corn Chip Melts

6-8 corn chips
2 tablespoons grated cheese

Arrange chips around edge of a plate or on grilling tray. Sprinkle with grated cheese.

MICROWAVE: Cook on HIGH for 20 seconds.

CONVENTIONAL: Grill until cheese bubbles and melts.

BOTH: Cool before serving. Melted cheese is very hot.

Bacon Buttie

$^1/_2$ rasher bacon or 1 slice ham
2 slices buttered bread (crusts removed)

MICROWAVE: Place bacon on plate and cover with luncheon wrap or plain brown paper. Do not use a paper towel as bacon sticks to it during cooking. Cook bacon 40-50 seconds on HIGH.

CONVENTIONAL: Grill bacon until crisp.

BOTH: Place cool bacon in fridge until cold. Place cold bacon between slices of buttered bread. Cut into four small triangles and serve.

Luncheon Sausage Surprises

1 slice luncheon sausage
2 toothpicks
required filling (ie. 'Surprise)
Choice of Surprises:
    prune, dried date, dried apricot, etc.
    cheese stick (cut from block)
    1 small marinated mussel
    $1/2$ pickled onion
    celery stick
    carrot stick
    slice apple, orange, pear etc
    banana stick
    small piece cold chicken
    piece pickled gherkin

Cut luncheon slice in half. Roll up chosen surprise inside luncheon and secure with toothpick.

HOT TIP: Variety is endless as you can use whatever is in the fridge. Toddlers will enjoy unwrapping the luncheon to find the surprise inside.

Plus all previous Finger Food Recipes.

Snacks for this Age.
All snacks mentioned to date are suitable.

Further Crusts . . .
Suggestions for Delicious Crusts Toppings suitable for this age:
    Toppings:
        peanut butter – alone or with hundreds and thousands
        honey – alone or with grated cheese
        jam – alone or with peanut butter

Index

**FIRST FOODS –
4-6 MONTHS**

Apple, Banana and Kumara
Delight   21
Apple Puree   16
Apricot, Peach and Pear Purees   16
Avocado and Banana Mash   22
Baby Rice   15
Banana Mush   17
Buttercup and Swede   18
Combination Vegie Soup   19
Creamy Vegies and Rice   20
Kumara and Carrot   18
Mashed Potato and Gravy   18
Pumpkin and Herb Soup   19
Pumpkin Smash   17
Robinsons and Fruit   17
Robinsons Royale   15
Suggested Finger Foods
(*See* Finger Foods and Snacks)
Summer Fruit Salad   22
Three Vegie Treat   19

**FURTHER PROGRESS –
6-9 MONTHS**

Apricot and Orange Vegies   29
Apricot Shake   45
Baby Roast Dinner   36
Banana Shake   43

Beef and Vegetable Stew   35
Beef Noodle Soup   38
Blackcurrant Jelly   42
Braised Liver and Baby Bacon   33
Cheeky Chicken   32
Cheesy Potatoes   40
Chicken and Sweetcorn Soup   39
Chicken and Vegetable Stew   34
Chicken Noodle Soup   38
Chocolate Semolina   41
Chocolate Shake   45
Combination Vegie Extra   28
Corned Beef and Vegetable Stew 35
Country Custard   44
Creamy Tutti-Frutti   44
Egg Yolk Supreme   28
Frozen Banana   42
Fruity Summer Salad   46
Ham and Vegetable Soup   38
Herbed Spaghetti Treat   36
Island Delight   43
Jolly Jelly   42
Kidney and Vegetable Surprise   31
Lamb and Vegetable Stew   34
Liver and Baby Bacon Delight   40
Liver and Vegetable Casserole   35
Meat and Vegetable Bake   33
Party Pumpkin   30
Pasta'n'Sauce   37

Perfect Parfait	46	Sizzling Sausage	62
Semolina Pudding	41	Spaghetti Babynaise	71
Simply Spaghetti	37	Strawberry Smoothie	75
Soft-Boiled Egg Yolk	28	Suggested Finger Foods	
Suggested Finger Foods		(*See* Finger Foods and Snacks)	
(*See* Finger Foods and Snacks)		Suggested Snacks	
Suggested Snacks		(*See* Finger Foods and Snacks)	
(*See* Finger Foods and Snacks)		Super Sundae	74
Tomato and Cheese Soup	39	Tasty Tuna and Rice	64
Vanilla Shake	45	Tiny Fish and Chips	73
Yoghurt and Fruit	43	Tomato Stuffing	67

GETTING THERE –
10-12 MONTHS

GRADUATION –
OVER 12 MONTHS

Apple Crumble	76	Advanced Creamy Egg Custard	101
Apricot Smoothie	75	Baked Custard	103
Baked Bean Bonanza	64	Boiled Egg and Soldiers	89
Banana Smoothie	75	Bread and Butter Pudding	103
Beef and Vegetable Casserole	70	Cheese Omelette	89
Chicken Casserole	70	Chocolate Goo	101
Chicken in Parsley Sauce	63	Coddled Egg	88
Chocolate Fruit Smoothie	76	Egg Foo Yong	91
Creamed Corn Surprise	66	Egg in a Dish	91
Fish Cake Feast	72	Fishburger Treat	96
Fruit Rabbit	73	Flummery	110
Hash Browns	66	Fruit Fritters	100
Irish Stew	65	Funny Face Eggs	92
Jelly Belly Delight	74	Hamburger Heaven	96
Liver and Rice	63	Icy Slicy	107
Macaroni and Cheese	68	Kitchen Hangi	97
Macaroni Cheese	69	Little Fruit Pudding	107
Peach Smoothie	75	Macaroni Custard	106
Potato Stuffing	68	Meat and Onion Fritters	100
Rice and Vegetables	65	Mini Hot Dog	97
Salmon Kedgeree	62	Mini Meat Kebabs	95

Omelette on Toast 90
Pancakes 108
Peanut Dip 94
Petite Pikelets 109
Pita Pocket 98
Rice Pudding 105
Savoury Egg Supreme 92
Savoury Pancakes 108
Scrambled Egg 88
Seafood Fritters 100
Semolina and Egg Custard 102
Semolina Supreme 102
Stuffed Sausage Supreme 94
Suggested Finger Foods
   (*See* Finger Foods and Snacks)
Suggested Snacks
   (*See* Finger Foods and Snacks)
Sweetcorn Omelette 90
Tuna Pie 93
Vegetable Fritters 99
Vegies and Dip 95

FINGER FOODS AND SNACKS

Bacon Buttie 113
Cheerios 52
Cheese Melts 54
Cheesy Biscuits 81
Cheesy Crackers 80
Corn Chip Melts 113
Crumpet Bites 111
Delicious Crusts 83
Drumstick Lick 23
Fish Fingers 53
French Toast Treat 54

Fruit in Muslin 23
Fruit Kebab 78
Fruit Platter 51
Fruits 56
Golden Baby Biscuits 82
Grated Goodies 48
Home-made Rusks 57
Ice cream in a Cone 79
Kumara Sticks 49
Luncheon Sausage Surprises 114
Mousetraps 83
Potato Wedges 50
Raw Fruit Platter 77
Raw Vegetable Platter 77
Roast Vegetables 48
Rollups 53
Sandwich Shapes 79
Senior Rollups 112
Simply Carrot 23
Stuffed Savoury Egg 112
Super Sandwiches 52
Vegetable Kebab 78
Vegetable Platter 51

PREPARATION AND STORAGE

Preparation 8
Storage – Free-flow Method 11
Storage – Fresh Food 10
Storage – Frozen Food 10

Your Notes